The PROVERBS 31 WOMAN

MIKE MURDOCK

TABLE OF CONTENTS

The Proverbs 31 Woman Copyright © 1994 by Mike Murdock
ISBN 1-56394-012-4
Published by Wisdom International
P. O. Box 99 • Denton, Texas 76202
Unless otherwise indicated, all Scripture quotations are taken from the *King James Version* of the Bible.

WHY I WROTE THIS BOOK.

The Proverbs 31 Woman.

What *man* would dare pen his thoughts, assessments and interpretation of such a controversial topic during these days of gender-bending, volatile and volcanic opinions?

Me.

But, then I couldn't help it. It has swept me like powerful undercurrents—toward intense hours of prayer, study and painful self-evaluation.

My revelations were strong enough to compel me to write this book—carefully, cautiously and sometimes dangerously.

My precious, godly and much loved mother asked only that I write it during her lifetime. Though she is now with Jesus, she remains the most logical picture I have of *The Proverbs 31 Woman.*

Every man longs for a *Proverbs 31 Woman.*

After my study, I'm almost certain that a true *Proverbs 31 Woman* probably would find me—unqualified.

Relax and *enjoy,*

Mike Murdock

❦ 1 ❦

SHE IS RARE.

"Who can find a virtuous woman? for her price is far above rubies" Proverbs 31:10.

She does exist.

She simply must be *found*.

She is one among thousands.

She is *not* average.

She is *not* common.

She is *not* typical.

She is not *easily* discovered.

What many women will *do*, she *refuses* to do.

What many women will *say*, she *refuses* to say.

What many women *wear*, she *refuses* to wear.

What makes many women angry, merely makes her more *thoughtful*.

What makes many women bitter, has increased her kindness.

Her *thoughts* are holy.

Her *motives* are pure.

Her *countenance* is cheerful.

She does not even respond to the *same kind of man* that many women find appealing.

This kind of woman is rarely found. Why?

It is a rare man who is *capable* of discerning her.

She Is Rare.

She Is The Proverbs 31 Woman.

➣ 2 ➣

IT IS A RARE MAN WHO IS CAPABLE OF DISCERNING HER.

———➤•◦•◄———

"Who can find a virtuous woman? for her price is far above rubies" Proverbs 31:10.

Every man secretly wishes for a Proverbs 31 Woman in his life.

Few can *qualify* for her.

Nabal, the foolish husband married to beautiful Abigail, never discerned how extraordinary she really was. It was King David who later sent for her, after Nabal's death. She became his wife.

Haman, the deceitful manipulator of the palace, never discerned Esther. He had no idea she was related to the man he hated, Mordecai.

The nearest kinsman did not discern Ruth. Boaz *did*, and she became the great grandmother of

David who ushered in the lineage of Jesus Christ.

Many claim that The Proverbs 31 Woman simply does not exist.

She does.

There are many true, pure and godly Proverbs 31 Women in our generation. But, only the qualified can discern who they really are.

It Is A Rare Man Who Is Capable Of Discerning Her.

She Is The Proverbs 31 Woman.

⇜ 3 ⇝

SHE REQUIRES PURSUIT.

"Who can find a virtuous woman? for her price is far above rubies" Proverbs 31:10.

The prostitute *pursues.*

The Proverbs 31 Woman *requires* pursuit.

The whorish woman stalks a man like a predator. She thrusts herself into his face. She pounds his door. She is telephoning men through the night.

She is unavoidable.

The Proverbs 31 Woman is different.

She is aware of her *difference.*

She is *accessible*, but, not unavoidable.

Boaz had to *return* for Ruth.

David had to *send* for Abigail.

The king had to *choose* Esther.

I love animals.

I've got a number of pets. Several years ago, I had an African lion, "KK." He was magnificent. He knew quite well that he was unlike my German Shepherd dogs. His reaction around them was almost one of disdain. His self-assurance was captivating.

Such is the self-assurance of The Proverbs 31 Woman.

She *knows* her value.

She is aware of her worth.

She *celebrates* her difference.

The worthy reach for her.

She Requires Pursuit.

She Is The Proverbs 31 Woman.

∽ 4 ∽

Money And Possessions Are Not Enough To Attract Her.

———◆———

"Who can find a virtuous woman? for her price is far above rubies" Proverbs 31:10.

I have heard hundreds of conversations among women regarding men they are dating, or their husband and his business. It is universally accepted that a man's financial status is an essential factor to the average woman preparing for marriage.

It is *normal* to desire security.

It is *normal* to desire to be under the covering of a successful man. If my daughter were getting married, I would be very concerned about *sowing* her life into the dream and future of a capable, competent and deserving man.

However, The Proverbs 31 Woman cannot be

bought.

It takes more than money, to get her attention. Why?

She is financially competent herself.

She is comfortable *with* money. She is confident *without* money.

She understands business.

Money And Possessions Are Not Enough To Attract Her.

She Is The Proverbs 31 Woman.

⋙ 5 ⋘

SHE PRODUCES FOR HER HUSBAND WHAT HIS MONEY FAILS TO PRODUCE.

⋙◦⋘

"Who can find a virtuous woman? for her price is far above rubies" Proverbs 31:10.

Price indicates value.

She is more valuable to her man *than his money.*

She brings to the marriage relationship *something greater than money.*

She benefits her husband consistently, in ways his business cannot satisfy.

This is a secret of her magnetism.

This keeps her man pursuing her.

This is what makes him come home on time in the evenings.

His business is burdensome.

His days are full.

His schedule is overwhelming.

But, he wants *her.*

His friends may leave.

His plans may fail.

His dream may crash.

But, She Is His World.

In her presence, he is proud.

In her presence, he is bold.

She Is The Only Place He Wants To Be.

She Produces For Her Husband What His Money Fails To Produce.

She Is The Proverbs 31 Woman.

⇒ 6 ⇐

SHE CAN BE TRUSTED.

—————⇒⇒-◉-⇐——————

"The heart of her husband doth safely trust in her, so that he shall have no need of spoil" Proverbs 31:11.

Everybody trusts somebody.

You *will* trust somebody, somewhere, at some time. I was explaining this to my son a few days ago—how to discern the *trustability* of another. When you are in the presence of someone who willingly and even cheerfully betrays the confidence of another, this indicates they will betray *your* confidence to another.

Every man trusts his woman.

That's how fleeing criminals are often caught. They reach back for a girlfriend they trust.

The wonder of The Proverbs 31 Woman is that her husband can trust in her...*safely*.

Eight Ways A Proverbs 31 Woman Can Be Trusted By Her Man

1. He can trust her with his *weaknesses.*

2. He can trust her with his *money.*

3. He can trust her with his *secrets.*

4. He can trust her with his *memories.*

5. He can trust her with his *fears.*

6. He can trust her to be faithful *sexually.*

7. He can trust her *around his friends.*

8. He can trust her *in his absence.*

"...she will richly satisfy his needs" (Proverbs 31:11 LB).

She Can Be Trusted.

She Is The Proverbs 31 Woman.

❧ 7 ❧

SHE WILL DO HIM GOOD.

⬤

"She will do him good" Proverbs 31:12.

The Proverbs 31 Woman brings out the best in her man.

She just does.

The worst often emerges when you are *alone*.

The best can come out of you when you have the right people around you as *catalysts*...unlocking the greatness lying dormant within you. "Two are better than one; because they have a good reward for their labour. Again, if two lie together, then they have heat: but how can one be warm alone?" (Ecclesiastes 4:8,11).

Everything created requires a connection.

Your eyes need a *view*.

Your ears require *sound.*

Your feet need for places to *walk.*

She will never become a *burden* to him.

She will never create *trouble* for him!

She will never be a *distraction* to him.

She will never be an *embarrassment* to him.

She will not *slow him down.*

She will never *stifle his greatness* within him.

She will never pull him *down.*

She will never *discourage his dreams.*

She is a *protection.*

She is a *multiplier.*

She Will Do Him Good.

She Is The Proverbs 31 Woman.

≫ 8 ≫

SHE DOES NOT HAVE A DANGEROUS SIDE TO HER.

⟫•◦•⟪

"She will do him good and not evil all the days of her life" Proverbs 31:11.

Her husband does not have to be cautious.

He does not have to be overly careful about what he says in her presence.

She will not use his unguarded words against him.

She is not a manipulator.

I have seen women that appeared to be "sugar sweetness." But, if you ever crossed them or failed to measure up to their expectation, their words could cut you to pieces. I have been astounded to see women change radically and suddenly, when someone failed to meet their expectations.

Most people have a *dangerous* side to them.

Not The Proverbs 31 Woman.

She does not *misinterpret* him.

She does not distort what he says.

She is not a manipulator.

She is not dangerous.

Ever.

She Does Not Have A Dangerous Side To Her.

She Is A Proverbs 31 Woman.

❧ 9 ❧

SHE LOVES TO WORK.

"She seeketh wool, and flax, and worketh willingly with her hands" Proverbs 31:13.

Many women *spend* money.

The Proverbs 31 Woman *invests* money.

Many women *want* money.

The Proverbs 31 Woman *understands* money.

Many women *seek* money.

The Proverbs 31 Woman *studies* money.

Many women *enjoy* money.

The Proverbs 31 Woman *earns* money.

Many women *hoard* money.

The Proverbs 31 Woman *sows* money.

You were created to produce. Increase is natural. Achieving is natural. It is unnatural to do nothing.

Almost everyone works. You must work to eat, to pay your bills, to pay for your medical insurance, and to buy your transportation.

But, The Proverbs 31 Woman *enjoys* work.

She *works*. That makes her *different*.

She works *willingly*. That makes her *unforgettable*.

The Proverbs 31 Woman doesn't whine on the job. She doesn't constantly proclaim to others how the low income of her husband requires that she work. She doesn't discuss with everyone how much she wishes she could quit working.

She knows that money is merely a reward for solving a problem, so she concentrates on solving problems for others.

She Loves To Work.

She Is The Proverbs 31 Woman.

⨋ 10 ⨋

SHE UNDERSTANDS THE NEED FOR CHANGE.

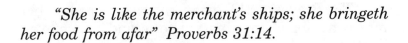

"She is like the merchant's ships; she bringeth her food from afar" Proverbs 31:14.

In ancient days, ships brought spices and a variety of foods from many different cultures of the world. It satisfied one of mankind's greatest needs: the need for variety and change.

The Proverbs 31 Woman is comfortable with this deep need for change.

She varies the taste and type of meals for her family.

She understands versatility. Changes.

She recognizes that *sameness destroys spontaneity* in her home and in her marriage.

Changes matter to her, too.

Variety excites her, also.

Most marriages experience a "rut" in some part of the relationship. Even love making can become boring. The sameness of daily routine often smothers us.

Same *words*.

Same *friends*.

Same *restaurants*.

Sameness can paralyze you.

The Proverbs 31 Woman knows the needs of her man can often change in a single second...she moves. She's ready...for those changes. She is as flexible as the ship that moves from port to port. You will not find her wearing the *same* gown every night, with the *same* missing button and the *same* torn pocket.

God loves diversity. I've got several different kinds of pheasants at my home. I have different kinds of animals. Sugar, our little white goat, loves to be rubbed on the head. Bambi, my pet deer, just loves to look and watch. My dogs love to be petted. My ducks and geese like to just run around honking and quacking. Everything God created has a different kind of need.

All of us have different needs.

The Proverbs 31 Woman Understands The Need For Change.

She Is The Proverbs 31 Woman.

~ 11 ~

SHE IS RESPONSIVE TO THE NEEDS OF OTHERS.

⇒►◦◄⇐

"She riseth also while it is yet night, and giveth meat to her household, and a portion to her maidens" *Proverbs 31:15.*

She arises early. She cooks breakfast. She is incredibly flexible.

Servanthood is a lost art these days. It takes *time*. It takes time to *learn*. The Proverbs 31 Woman is not sitting in the corner of the expensive restaurant... waiting to be served. She is not looking down her nose condescendingly at servants and maids. She produces. She moves. She accommodates.

She Is Responsive To The Needs Of Others.

She Is A Proverbs 31 Woman.

"She riseth also while it is yet night, and giveth meat to her household, and a portion to her maidens" ***Proverbs 31:15.***

~ 12 ~

SHE IS AN EARLY RISER.

———————➤◦◄———————

"She riseth also while it is yet night, and giveth meat to her household, and a portion to her maidens" *Proverbs 31:15.*

The Proverbs 31 Woman values her time.

The average woman does not carry a *Time-Management* Notebook. She has lipstick, powder, mirror, nail polish...not a Day Planner!

Some people lose hundreds of hours in watching soap operas, talking to friends on the telephone or just sitting around the house. Many do not have a strong sense of purpose. They are not focused on their Assignment. Those who will waste their time, will eventually waste your time, too.

But, The Proverbs 31 Woman is *different.*

Her *time* matters.

Her *schedule* is precious.

She has *focus*.

She has a *plan*.

She gets *results*.

She is very sensitive about *mastering a day*.

She Is An Early Riser.

She Is The Proverbs 31 Woman.

⚋ 13 ⚋

SHE IS A PROBLEM SOLVER, NOT A PROBLEM.

────────◆─◆─◆────────

"She riseth also while it is yet night, and giveth meat to her household, and a portion to her maidens" *Proverbs 31:15.*

She notices the needs of *others*.

She moves. She contributes. She cooperates.

She understands schedules. She is flexible.

She adapts, and accommodates the changing plans and schedules of those to whom she has been assigned.

No whining. No griping. No yelling.

She Is A Problem Solver, Not A Problem.

She Is The Proverbs 31 Woman.

"She considereth a field, and buyeth it: with the fruit of her hands she planteth a vineyard" Proverbs 31:16.

⮐ 14 ⮐

SHE IS COMFORTABLE AND COMPETENT IN THE WORLD OF BUSINESS.

⮕⬥⬥⬅

"She considereth a field, and buyeth it: with the fruit of her hands she planteth a vineyard" *Proverbs 31:16.*

She has learned the *language* of business.

She understands the Laws of Increase.

Esther was thoroughly trained in the rules of protocol.

She was well-versed in policies and procedures.

Ruth was comfortable in the fields of Boaz. She got involved with his *business* before she got involved with *him*. She *understood his business before she understood him.*

Abigail understood Nabal's business. That's why she could feed several hundred men in a single day without being advised weeks ahead of time.

I valued my own mother because she interrogated my father constantly concerning the flow of his ministry, his business transactions and the decisions he was making. Sometimes, my father did not want to tell her certain aspects. He's closed-mouthed. But she insisted and on many occasions made marvelous contributions.

Many women do not have a thorough grasp of her husband's business. She does not understand his decisions. She does not even understand why he is emptied at the end of a day.

The Proverbs 31 Woman understands the mind and heart of an achiever.

She Is Comfortable And Competent In The World Of Business.

She Is A Proverbs 31 Woman.

～ 15 ～

SHE IS CAUTIOUS IN DECISION MAKING.

"She considereth a field, and buyeth it" Proverbs *31:16.*

The Proverbs 31 Woman is not impulsive. She does not awaken with a "spiritual dream" and purchase some strange business suddenly. She gathers data. She *considers* a field. *Then,* buys it.

She does not make *quick* decisions.

She makes *right* decisions.

Her decisions create *long-term* gain. "She shall rejoice *in time to come*" (Proverbs 31:25). Sam Walton, the billionaire, often said he would never invest in a company for where it would be in 18 months, but where it would be in ten years.

She Is Cautious In Decision Making.

She Is The Proverbs 31 Woman.

"She girdeth her loins with strength, and strengtheneth her arms" Proverbs 31:17.

~ 16 ~

SHE IS PHYSICALLY FIT.

"She girdeth her loins with strength, and strengtheneth her arms" Proverbs 31:17.

Health matters to The Proverbs 31 Woman.

Many women want to *look* healthy.

The Proverbs 31 Woman wants to *be* healthy. She does whatever it takes to "strengthen" her life and body to stay healthy. Exercise matters to her. Food choices are important to her.

That's why she stays cheerful. One famed doctor says, "I have yet to treat anyone for depression who was physically fit."

She Is Physically Fit.

She Is The Proverbs 31 Woman.

"She perceiveth that her merchandise is good" Proverbs 31:18.

❧ 17 ❧

SHE DOES NOT REQUIRE CONSTANT REASSURANCE OF HER SELF-WORTH.

"She perceiveth that her merchandise is good"
Proverbs 31:18.

She knows her worth.

She does not need for others to reassure her.

She does not require men to be incessant cheerleaders in her life. Her husband is not always needed to hold her hand and speak effusive compliments, even though he praises her.

She walks in total peace.

She exudes excellence.

She puts quality into her work.

Her work puts quality back into her. "But let every man prove his own work, and then shall he have rejoicing in himself alone, and not in another" (Galatians 6:4).

She Does Not Require Constant Reassurance Of Her Self-Worth.

She Is The Proverbs 31 Woman.

❧ 18 ❧

SHE WILLINGLY INVESTS EXTRA TIME IN THE THINGS THAT REALLY MATTER.

---◆◆◆---

"Her candle goeth not out by night" Proverbs 31:18.

Great things require time. *Extra time.*

It takes time to *plan.*

It takes time to *learn.*

Great things rarely come easily. As I look back at the many books and songs I've written and published, not one has really come easy. The results are thrilling, however, when you willingly go the extra mile.

That's what makes The Proverbs 31 Woman so unforgettable.

Her candle stays lit.

Others are asleep.

But, she is still working.

Her productivity is worth her extra time.

Few want to go this extra mile.

Champions Do Things They Hate To Create Something Else They Love.

The Proverbs 31 Woman knows that sowing the Seed of Time in what she loves will bring more joy than she has ever imagined.

She Willingly Invests Extra Time In The Things That Really Matter.

She Is The Proverbs 31 Woman.

☙ 19 ☙

SHE KNOWS THE TOOLS NECESSARY TO COMPLETE HER TASKS.

―――▶❖◀―――

"She layeth her hands to the spindle, and her hands hold the distaff" Proverbs 31:19.

Jobs require appropriate equipment.

The Proverbs 31 Woman knows this. She is *knowledgeable* of necessary equipment to do her job, has the *willingness* to purchase it and the *determination* to use it!

She has not tried to cut corners on quality. She investes in quality equipment. She uses it.

Her tools are important to her.

She Knows The Tools Necessary To Complete Her Tasks.

She Is The Proverbs 31 Woman.

"She stretcheth out her hand to the poor; yea, she reacheth forth her hands to the needy" Proverbs 31:20.

～ 20 ～

SHE REACTS TO THE PAIN OF OTHERS.

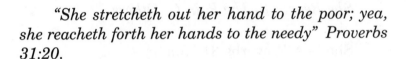

"She stretcheth out her hand to the poor; yea, she reacheth forth her hands to the needy" Proverbs 31:20.

She is *observant.*

She is *compassionate.*

She *feels.*

She has not *withdrawn* from the flow of life around her.

She has not *shielded* herself from damaged people.

She has *reached* out toward them. She is *involved.* She is confident that her love and compassion can *make a difference.*

She wants to be the *solution* to their problem.

Many women focus on having their needs met.

The Proverbs 31 Woman focuses on meeting the needs of others.

Some women want servants.

The Proverbs 31 Woman wants to serve.

She Reacts To The Pain Of Others.

She Is A Proverbs 31 Woman.

❧ 21 ❧

SHE WILLINGLY ASSOCIATES WITH THOSE LESS FORTUNATE.

―――❖―――

"She stretcheth out her hand to the poor; yea, she reacheth forth her hands to the needy" Proverbs 31:20.

The Proverbs 31 Woman is prosperous.

She is emotionally secure.

She has a home. Servants. Land. Business. Social status. A loving husband. Obedient children.

Yet, she is not aloof or distant with the poor.

She has a servant's heart. *That's why she knows what others are feeling around her.*

Some women are social climbers. I read a lot of magazines, especially women's magazines. They are so well written and quite revealing about motives behind behavior. Almost every major article is focused on climbing the corporate ladder, getting more perks from the boss, or dealing with sexual harassment. Few ever address how to serve, how to heal, or how to restore the broken.

That's why The Proverbs 31 Woman is so magnetic.

She Willingly Associates With Those Less Fortunate.

She Is The Proverbs 31 Woman.

∽ 22 ∽

SHE ANTICIPATES CHANGES.

—————◆◦◀——

"She is not afraid of the snow for her household: for all her household are clothed with scarlet" *Proverbs 31:21.*

Life is a collection of surprises.

One single event can throw an entire year into disarray. One hour can dramatically affect your life.

The Proverbs 31 Woman is undisturbed by these changes. Even the weather. Obviously, there is more meaning to this scripture than the discussion of snow.

She prepares for new seasons.

She thinks ahead.

She does not wait for her husband's involvement.

She does not sit idly waiting for her children to have problems.

She sees problems before they arrive.

She lives *prepared.* This reveals her philosophy toward life, her family and her tasks.

She Anticipates Changes.

She Is A Proverbs 31 Woman.

❧ 23 ❧

SHE INVESTS IN HER APPEARANCE.

———————

"She maketh herself coverings of tapestry; her clothing is silk and purple" Proverbs 31:22.

This is quite interesting—she *covers* herself.

That makes her rare indeed! Some women are afraid that their intelligence will go undiscovered, their sincerity undetected, their integrity undiscerned; so they *package their body* to create a *relationship.*

The Proverbs 7 harlot dresses to ignite *lust.*

The Proverbs 31 Woman dresses to ignite *love.*

The Proverbs 7 harlot stimulates *pursuit.*

The Proverbs 31 Woman inspires *protection.*

You are a walking message system.

Your clothing telegraphs the message.

When Naomi was mentoring Ruth, she told her to wash her hair, change clothes and package herself, to make herself desirable, for the man she desired.

If you want to be desired, you must make yourself desirable.

A good appearance does not just happen.

A good appearance is not an accident.

A good appearance is not always easy.

A good appearance is not always convenient.

It is time-consuming. It requires the investment of time and money.

Yet, it is part of her mystery. It is one of the secrets of satisfying and stimulating The Uncommon Man.

The Proverbs 31 Woman cares, and it shows.

She Invests In Her Appearance.

She Is A Proverbs 31 Woman.

❧ 24 ❧

SHE PROTECTS THE FOCUS OF HER HUSBAND.

"Her husband is known in the gates, when he sitteth among the elders of the land" Proverbs 31:23.

Esther chose to honor the focus of the king, even though her life was at stake.

Ruth did not give an ultimatum to Boaz about marriage. He made the decision himself.

Abigail did not trouble Nabal about her conversation with David until *after* the crisis.

Some women rarely celebrate or even notice their husband's focus at any given time. They want to talk shopping when the Super Bowl is on television. They want to discuss the children when he has just had a major crisis on his job.

The Proverbs 31 Woman is *different*.

She helps her man keep *his focus.*

You see, her husband is respected.

He is accepted. Celebrated. Treasured.

His wisdom is recognized by others.

She participates in that greatness.

She removes his distractions.

She adapts to his schedule.

She Protects The Focus Of Her Husband.

She Is The Proverbs 31 Woman.

⤳ 25 ⤳

She Finishes What She Starts.

⟪⟫

"She maketh fine linen, and selleth it; and delivereth girdles unto the merchant" Proverbs 31:24.

She *makes*...her product

She *sells*...her product.

She *delivers*...her product.

She completes what she starts.

She has the spirit of a *Finisher*.

Champions are Finishers.

Paul said, "I have *finished* my course" (2 Timothy 4:7).

Solomon *finished* the temple.

Jesus cried out, "It is *finished*."

Great people are follow-through people.

The Proverbs 31 Woman is the Master of Follow Through.

Some women *begin* projects.

The Proverbs 31 Woman *finishes* projects.

Jesus said, "No man, having put his hand to the plough, and looking back, is fit for the kingdom of God" (Luke 9:62).

The Proverbs 31 Woman will not start a project unless she is committed to its completion.

She Finishes What She Starts.

She Is A Proverbs 31 Woman.

❧ 26 ❧

SHE ONLY DISCUSSES WHAT SHE KNOWS.

＊＊＊＊＊

"She openeth her mouth with Wisdom; and in her tongue is the law of kindness" Proverbs 31:26.

It is normal to open your mouth.

It is abnormal to open it with *wisdom*.

Everybody has an opinion. Few articulate it well.

When the Proverbs 31 Woman speaks, it pays to listen.

She is decided, so she is *decisive*.

She is persuaded, so she *persuades*.

She is convinced, so she *convinces*.

She is motivated, so she *motivates*.

She is energized, so she *energizes*.

She is informed, so she *informs*.

She Only Discusses What She Knows.

She Is A Proverbs 31 Woman.

⇜ 27 ⇝

SHE IS CONSISTENT IN HER BEHAVIOR, REGARDLESS OF THE CIRCUMSTANCES.

"She openeth her mouth with Wisdom; and in her tongue is the law of kindness" Proverbs 31:26.

Many women are skilled in *public.*

Many women have spontaneous, sparkling personalities.

Many can summon a quick smile and the *appearance* of warmth at a moment's notice.

But, The Proverbs 31 Woman does not change her personality to manipulate a situation.

In her mouth the Law of Kindness rules.

From her mouth, kindness flows.

Her words *never* destroy.

Her words *never* tear down.

Her words *never* paralyze.

Her words are *life*.

Her words bring *hope*.

Her words *restore*.

Her words *heal*.

Her words *mend*.

She Is Consistent In Her Behavior, Regardless Of The Circumstances.

She Is A Proverbs 31 Woman.

～ 28 ～

SHE CONTINUALLY EVALUATES THE BEHAVIOR OF HER HOUSEHOLD.

"She looketh well to the ways of her household, and eateth not of the bread of idleness" Proverbs *31:27.*

She is not easily deceived.

She is not a pushover.

She knows her turf.

She dominates "her" world.

She has decided the productivity of her home.

She knows her children's homework.

She knows her children's friends.

She examines.

She observes.

She pursues information.

The true Proverbs 31 Woman will reach under the mattress of her 16-year-old son's bed, and find the magazines he's trying to hide.

She listens carefully to what her daughter says on the phone to her friends.

She knows the subjects most difficult for her children in school.

She is committed to the success of her family. She knows what their problems are.

She Continually Evaluates The Behavior Of Her Household.

She Is A Proverbs 31 Woman.

∼ 29 ∼

HER CHILDREN ENJOY HER.

———————>∙0∙<———————

"Her children arise up, and call her blessed; her husband also, and he praiseth her" Proverbs 31:28.

The Queen of Sheba observed to Solomon, "Happy are thy men, happy are these thy servants, which stand continually before thee" (1 Kings 10:8).

The children of The Proverbs 31 Woman do the same.

They *respect* her.

They *love* her.

They *enjoy* her.

They call her *blessed*.

This reveals much about her philosophy of correction and discipline.

She is *not* a screamer.

She does *not* lose control.

She does *not* explode with uncontrollable anger.

She *understands* discipline.

Her Seeds of kindness have produced her desired harvest.

Her Children Enjoy Her.

She Is A Proverbs 31 Woman.

∞ 30 ∞

HER HUSBAND PRAISES HER.

—————◆————

"Her children arise up and call her blessed; her husband also, and he praiseth her" Proverbs 31:28.

Some months ago, I sat in a beautiful office listening to a lady brag on herself. Her husband sat there quietly, not saying a word. She poured out a stream of compliments such as, "You'll never find another woman like me. I am one-of-a-kind. God blessed you when I walked into your life."

Of course, I realized something inside her was screaming for attention—struggling for significance. He had nothing to say.

You see, "Let another man praise thee, and not thine own mouth; a stranger, and not thine own lips" (Proverbs 27:2).

Quiet confidence is magnetic to men.

Desperation is a turn-off.

Any worthy man discerns those who have helped create his success.

The Proverbs 31 Woman is honored, loved and valued by the man whose life she has enhanced.

Her Husband Praises Her.

She Is A Proverbs 31 Woman.

❧ 31 ❧

SHE FEARS THE LORD.

⟶✦❖✦⟵

"...a woman that feareth the Lord, she shall be praised" Proverbs 31:30.

She fears God.

This is why she hates evil.

"The fear of the Lord is to hate evil: pride, and arrogancy, and the evil way, and the froward mouth" (Proverbs 8:13).

Alcohol is deadly, so you will not find it in her glass.

Cigarettes are cancerous, so you will not find one in her mouth.

Drugs are destructive, so you will not find them in her purse.

Cursing is blasphemous, so you will not hear it from her lips.

Gambling bankrupts, so do not look for her in the casino.

Ungodly companions pollute, so do not look for her in their company.

My mother hated evil in any form. When I was ten years old, she forced me to call my friends back at school and confess to them a lie I had told. I still remember that humiliation and embarrassment!! She is a perfect photograph of integrity to me to this very day.

The Proverbs 31 Woman loathes and despises anything unlike her God.

She Fears The Lord.

She Is A Proverbs 31 Woman.

The Proverbs 31 Woman Is The Closest Thing To God A Child Will Ever Know.

The Proverbs 31 Woman Is The Closest Thing To Heaven A Man Will Ever Experience On Earth.

ORDER FORM THE MIKE MURDOCK WISDOM LIBRARY
(All books paperback unless indicated otherwise.)

QTY	CODE	BOOK TITLE	USA	TOTAL
	B01	WISDOM FOR WINNING	$10	
	B02	5 STEPS OUT OF DEPRESSION	$ 3	
	B03	THE SEX TRAP	$ 3	
	B04	10 LIES PEOPLE BELIEVE ABOUT MONEY	$ 3	
	B05	FINDING YOUR PURPOSE IN LIFE	$ 3	
	B06	CREATING TOMORROW THROUGH SEED-FAITH	$ 3	
	B07	BATTLE TECHNIQUES FOR WAR WEARY SAINTS	$ 3	
	B08	ENJOYING THE WINNING LIFE	$ 3	
	B09	FOUR FORCES/GUARANTEE CAREER SUCCESS	$ 3	
	B10	THE BRIDGE CALLED DIVORCE	$ 3	
	B11	DREAM SEEDS	$ 9	
	B12	YOUNG MINISTERS HANDBOOK	$20	
	B13	SEEDS OF WISDOM ON DREAMS AND GOALS	$ 3	
	B14	SEEDS OF WISDOM ON RELATIONSHIPS	$ 3	
	B15	SEEDS OF WISDOM ON MIRACLES	$ 3	
	B16	SEEDS OF WISDOM ON SEED-FAITH	$ 3	
	B17	SEEDS OF WISDOM ON OVERCOMING	$ 3	
	B18	SEEDS OF WISDOM ON HABITS	$ 3	
	B19	SEEDS OF WISDOM ON WARFARE	$ 3	
	B20	SEEDS OF WISDOM ON OBEDIENCE	$ 3	
	B21	SEEDS OF WISDOM ON ADVERSITY	$ 3	
	B22	SEEDS OF WISDOM ON PROSPERITY	$ 3	
	B23	SEEDS OF WISDOM ON PRAYER	$ 3	
	B24	SEEDS OF WISDOM ON FAITH-TALK	$ 3	
	B25	SEEDS OF WISDOM ONE YEAR DEVOTIONAL	$10	
	B26	THE GOD BOOK	$10	
	B27	THE JESUS BOOK	$10	
	B28	THE BLESSING BIBLE	$10	
	B29	THE SURVIVAL BIBLE	$10	
	B30	THE TEEN'S TOPICAL BIBLE	$ 6	
	B30L	THE TEEN'S TOPICAL BIBLE (LEATHER)	$20	
	B31	THE ONE-MINUTE TOPICAL BIBLE	$10	
	B32	THE MINISTER'S TOPICAL BIBLE	$ 6	
	B33	THE BUSINESSMAN'S TOPICAL BIBLE	$ 6	
	B33L	THE BUSINESSMAN'S TOPICAL BIBLE (LEATHER)	$20	
	B34L	THE GRANDPARENT'S TOPICAL BIBLE (LEATHER)	$20	
	B35	THE FATHER'S TOPICAL BIBLE	$ 6	
	B35L	THE FATHER'S TOPICAL BIBLE (LEATHER)	$20	
	B36	THE MOTHER'S TOPICAL BIBLE	$ 6	
	B36L	THE MOTHER'S TOPICAL BIBLE (LEATHER)	$20	
	B37	THE NEW CONVERT'S TOPICAL BIBLE	$15	
	B38	THE WIDOW'S TOPICAL BIBLE	$ 6	
	B39	THE DOUBLE DIAMOND PRINCIPLE	$ 9	
	B40	WISDOM FOR CRISIS TIMES	$ 9	
	B41	THE GIFT OF WISDOM (VOLUME ONE)	$ 8	
	B42	ONE-MINUTE BUSINESSMAN'S DEVOTIONAL	$10	
	B43	ONE-MINUTE BUSINESSWOMAN'S DEVOTIONAL	$10	
	B44	31 SECRETS FOR CAREER SUCCESS	$10	
	B45	101 WISDOM KEYS	$ 7	
	B46	31 FACTS ABOUT WISDOM	$ 7	
	B47	THE COVENANT OF THE FIFTY-EIGHT BLESSINGS	$ 8	
	B48	31 KEYS TO A NEW BEGINNING	$ 7	
	B49	THE PROVERBS 31 WOMAN	$ 7	
	B50	ONE-MINUTE POCKET BIBLE FOR THE ACHIEVER	$ 5	
	B51	ONE-MINUTE POCKET BIBLE FOR FATHERS	$ 5	
	B52	ONE-MINUTE POCKET BIBLE FOR MOTHERS	$ 5	

MAIL TO: **DR. MIKE MURDOCK •THE WISDOM TRAINING CENTER • P.O. BOX 99 • DENTON, TX 76202**
(940) 891-1400 OR USA CALL TOLL FREE 1-888-WISDOM-1

Qty	Code	Book Title	USA	Total
	B53	One-Minute Pocket Bible For Teenagers	$ 5	
	B54	One-Minute Devotional (hardback)	$14	
	B55	20 Keys To A Happier Marriage	$ 3	
	B56	How To Turn Mistakes Into Miracles	$ 3	
	B57	31 Secrets Of The Unforgettable Woman	$ 9	
	B58	Mentor's Manna On Attitude	$ 3	
	B59	The Making Of A Champion	$ 6	
	B60	One-Minute Pocket Bible For Men	$ 5	
	B61	One-Minute Pocket Bible For Women	$ 5	
	B62	One-Minute Pocket Bible/Bus.Professionals	$ 5	
	B63	One-Minute Pocket Bible For Truckers	$ 5	
	B64	7 Obstacles To Abundant Success	$ 3	
	B65	Born To Taste The Grapes	$ 3	
	B66	Greed, Gold And Giving	$ 3	
	B67	Gift Of Wisdom For Champions	$ 8	
	B68	Gift Of Wisdom For Achievers	$ 8	
	B69	Wisdom Keys For A Powerful Prayer Life	$ 3	
	B70	Gift Of Wisdom For Mothers	$ 8	
	B71	Wisdom - God's Golden Key To Success	$ 7	
	B72	The Greatest Success Habit On Earth	$ 3	
	B73	The Mentor's Manna On Abilities	$ 3	
	B74	The Assignment: Dream/Destiny #1	$10	
	B75	The Assignment: Anointing/Adversity #2	$10	
	B76	The Mentor's Manna On The Assignment	$ 3	
	B77	The Gift Of Wisdom For Fathers	$ 8	
	B78	The Mentor's Manna On The Secret Place	$ 3	
	B79	The Mentor's Manna On Achievement	$ 3	
	B80	The Double Diamond Daily Devotional	$12	
	B81	The Mentor's Manna On Adversity	$ 3	
	B82	31 Reasons People Do Not Receive Their Financial Harvest	$12	
	B83	The Gift Of Wisdom For Wives	$ 8	
	B84	The Gift Of Wisdom For Husbands	$ 8	
	B85	The Gift Of Wisdom For Teenagers	$ 8	
	B86	The Gift Of Wisdom For Leaders	$ 8	
	B87	The Gift Of Wisdom For Graduates	$ 8	
	B88	The Gift Of Wisdom For Brides	$ 8	
	B89	The Gift Of Wisdom For Grooms	$ 8	
	B90	The Gift Of Wisdom For Ministers	$ 8	
	B91h	The Leadership Secrets Of Jesus (hdbk)	$15	
	B92	Secrets Of The Journey (Vol. 1)	$ 5	
	B93	Secrets Of The Journey (Vol. 2)	$ 5	
	B94	Secrets Of The Journey (Vol. 3)	$ 5	
	B95	Secrets Of The Journey (Vol. 4)	$ 5	

❏ CASH ❏ CHECK ❏ MONEY ORDER

❏ CREDIT CARD # ❏ VISA ❏ MC ❏ AMEX

EXPIRATION DATE *SORRY NO C.O.D.'s*

Signature _____

TOTAL PAGE 2	$
TOTAL PAGE 1	$
*ADD SHIPPING 10% USA/20% OTHERS	$
CANADA CURRENCY DIFFERENCE ADD20%	$
TOTAL ENCLOSED	$

PLEASE PRINT

Name _____

Address _____

State   Zip

City _____

Phone (___) ___ - ___

MIKE MURDOCK

- Began full-time evangelism at the age of 19, which has continued for 34 years.

- Has traveled and spoken to more than 14,000 audiences in 36 countries, including East Africa, the Orient, and Europe.

- Noted author of 115 books, including best sellers, *Wisdom for Winning, Dream Seeds and The Double Diamond Principle.*

- Created the popular *"Wisdom Topical Bible"* series for Businessmen, Mothers, Fathers, Teenagers, and the *One-Minute Pocket Bible.*

- Has composed more than 5,600 songs such as *I Am Blessed, You Can Make It, and Jesus Just The Mention Of Your Name,* recorded by many artists.

- Is the Founder of the Wisdom Center in Dallas, Texas.

- Has a weekly television program called *"Wisdom Keys With Mike Murdock".*

- He has appeared often on TBN, CBN, Oral Roberts and other television network programs.

- Is a Founding Trustee on the Board of International Charismatic Bible Ministries founded by Oral Roberts.

- Has seen over 3,400 accept the call into full-time ministry under his ministry.

- Has embraced his Assignment: *Pursuing... Possessing... And Publishing The Wisdom Of God To Heal The Broken In This Generation.*

THE MINISTRY

1 **Wisdom Books & Literature** -115 best-selling Wisdom books and Teaching tapes that teach the Wisdom of God to thousands.

2 **Church Crusades** - Multitudes are ministered to in crusades and seminars throughout America in "The Uncommon Wisdom Conferences."

3 **Music Ministry** - Millions have been blessed by the anointed songwriting and singing of Mike Murdock, who has written over 5,600 songs.

4 **Television** - "Wisdom Keys With Mike Murdock," a nationally-syndicated weekly television program.

5 **The Wisdom Center** - Where Dr. Murdock holds annual Schools of Ministry for those training for a more excellent ministry.

6 **Schools of the Holy Spirit** - Mike Murdock hosts Schools of the Holy Spirit to mentor believers on the Person and companionship of the Holy Spirit.

7 **Schools of Wisdom** - Each year Mike Murdock hosts Schools of Wisdom for those who want personalized and advanced training for achieving "The Uncommon Dream."

8 **Missionary Ministry** - Dr. Murdock's overseas outreaches to 36 countries have included crusades to East Africa, South America, and Europe.

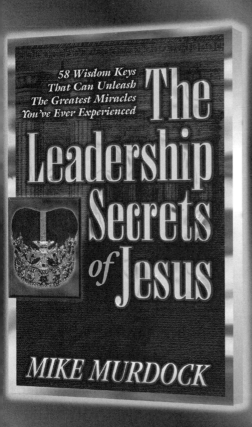

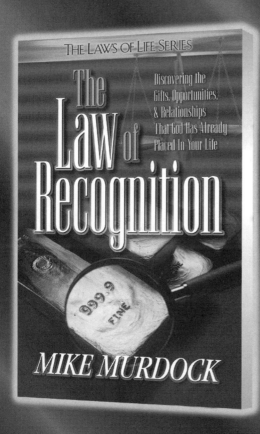

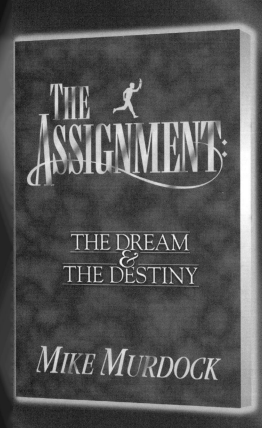

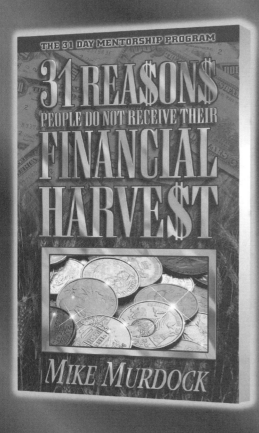

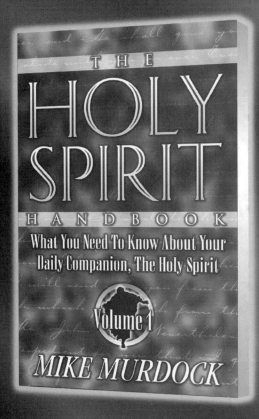

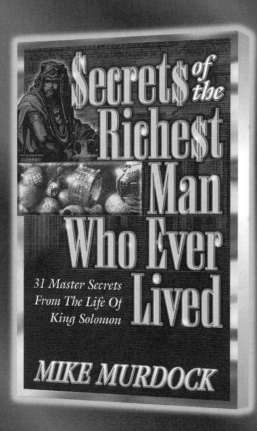

1000 Times More.

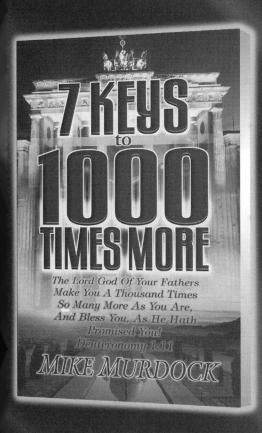

7 KEYS to 1000 TIMES MORE

The Lord God Of Your Fathers Make You A Thousand Times So Many More As You Are, And Bless You, As He Hath Promised You!
Deuteronomy 1:11

MIKE MURDOCK

▶ **52 Things God Wants To Increase In Your Life!** ...p.114-122

▶ **7 Reasons God Wants To Increase Your Finances!** ...p.15-16

▶ **6 Qualities Of Uncommon Love!**...p.19

▶ **40 Facts You Must Know About The Uncommon Dream God Places Within You**...p.28-40

▶ **The Greatest Success Law I Ever Discovered**...p.46

▶ **14 Keys In Developing Your Daily Success Routine!**...p.84-85

▶ **58 Important Facts About Obedience!**...p.65-80

▶ **12 Facts About Your Life Assignment!**...p.39-42

and much more!

It's time to push the limits on your personal increase. God wants to multiply you exceedingly in every area of your life. God wants you to live The Uncommon Life and that life comes when you set your faith to reach 1000 Times More. In this exciting teaching, Dr. Mike Murdock spells out the qualities of an achiever who will walk in multiplication and increase. All of the pitfalls, principles, and rewards are covered in this concise message and you will soon be moving forward in the direction of the greatest season harvest you've ever known.

Available also on six tapes for only $30!

B-104
$10⁰⁰
Wisdom Is The Principal Thing

The Wisdom Center ▪ P.O. Box 99 ▪ Denton, Texas ▪ 76202
940-891-1400 ▪ Fax: 940-891-4500 ▪ www.mikemurdock.com

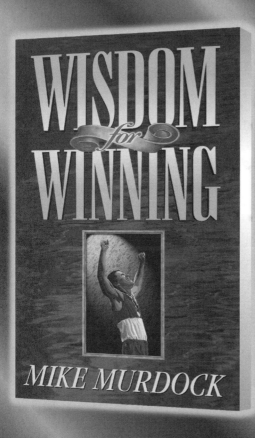